CUNTRY

CUNTRY by Kristin Sanders
Published by Trembling Pillow Press
New Orleans, LA
ISBN-13: 978-0-9964757-5-4
Copyright © 2017 Kristin Sanders

All Rights Reserved. No part of this book may be reproduced in any form without permission from the publisher with the exception of brief passages cited or for educational purposes. Reproduction for commercial use is prohibited except by permission of the author.

Typesetting and Design: Megan Burns
Cover Design: JS Makkos
Author Photo: Jill Goodwin
Copyedit: Kia Alice Groom

CUNTRY

Kristin Sanders

"HAMLET: Do you think I meant country matters?
OPHELIA: I think nothing, my lord.
HAMLET: That's a fair thought to lie between maids' legs."

-Shakespeare, *Hamlet* (III.II.116-18)

"Am I pornography?"

-Katherine Angel, *Unmastered*

Table of Contents

"Inside *The Spell of the Sensuous*…"	13
"My childhood was porn…"	15
"I seek out images…"	16
How to Write a Country Song	17
Chattahoochee Sung By Alan Jackson	18
Figure 1.	19
"When I tell people…"	20
"Or maybe I went to Nashville because…"	21
"My therapist during my one year in Nashville…"	22
What the Cowgirls Do Sung By Vince Gill	23
"I don't believe I had any innocence …"	24
"My sister says she grew up believing…"	25
Dead Dog Country Song	26
The First Country Song	27
CUNFESSION	29
Figure 2.	30
"I let my imagination lead me…"	31
"Look, I do want you to read this, though…"	32
Shameless Sung By Garth Brooks	33
"I start looking at cum shot videos…"	34
Fancy Sung By Reba McEntire	35

Daddy's Money Sung By Ricochet	37
Country Song of Thanks	38
Trashy Women Sung By Confederate Railroad	40
Figure 3.	41
I Feel Lucky Sung By Mary Chapin Carpenter	42
"When I was in high school…"	43
Working 9 to 5 Sung By Dolly Parton	44
Rock My World (Little Country Girl) Sung By Brooks & Dunn	45
"In high school, because it was 2001…"	46
XXX's and OOO'x (An American Girl) Sung By Trisha Yearwood	47
The Fireman Sung By George Strait	48
Figure 4.	49
John Deere Green Sung By Joe Diffie	50
Callin' Baton Rouge Sung By Garth Brooks	51
Jolene Sung By Dolly Parton	52
Something in Red Sung By Lorrie Morgan	53
Figure 5.	54
Pickup Man Sung By Joe Diffie	55
"I've never been raped, but…"	56
A Little Too Late Sung By Tanya Tucker	57
"I hate to write this…"	58
"I watch "Dr. Piss"…"	59
"I position myself as a voyeur…"	60

"I can go weeks or months without…"	61
"I've never had a crush on a porn star before…"	62
"I've never wanted fucking to hurt…"	63
Old Flames Have New Names Sung By Mark Chesnutt	64
Country Song of Regret	65
Figure 6.	67
Maybe It Was Memphis Sung By Pam Tillis	68
Angry Woman Country Song	69
Should've Been A Cowboy Sung By Toby Keith	71
Figure 7.	73
I Love The Way You Love Me Sung By John Michael Montgomery	74
"COUNTRY" WITHOUT THE O:	75
Independence Day Sung By Martina McBride	76
"I must be honest now…"	77
"There was one time when I came…"	78
Internet Porn Country Song	79
The Last Country Song	82

Notes
Acknowledgments

Inside *The Spell of the Sensuous* is a note in my own handwriting, a to-do list from a few years ago. The list is: 1) stop watching porn 2) write country songs 3) learn guitar 4) lose weight 5) move to Nashville 6) stop getting fucked. Note, too, that I had underlined:

> *Like the mountains of the four directions, and like the other animals, and the plants, humans are themselves one of the Wind's dwelling places, one of its multiple centers, and just as we are nourished and influenced by the Air at large, so do our actions and thoughts affect the Air in turn. The individual, that is, is not passive with respect to the Holy Wind; rather <u>she participates in it</u>, as one of its organs. <u>Her own desire and intent (her own interior Wind) participates directly in the life of the invisible Wind all around her, and hence can engage and subtly influence events in all the surrounding terrain.</u>*

My childhood was porn and country songs: sexuality birthed from the lips of a stranger's hairless vulva on the screen, or in the bed of a boy's raised truck—my desire dry-humping my body into the bad world.

The dream: to move from California to Nashville, to right country songs, to fix, rub against rough edges, to come, to give the cuntry object back her voice.

I seek out images of women sucking cocks, women with gaping mouth holes, gaping ass holes, vaginal lips spread apart by a man's hands or the woman's own, images of women with dicks in their holes, all of their holes, two dicks in one hole, images of women's breasts grabbed, sucked, hit by a stiff dick, slapped, the nipples pinched, bit, the breasts tied by rope, two round sockets about to burst, images of women licking another woman's vulva, sticking the sharp nails at the tips of her fingers into the vagina of another woman, images of a woman encircled by a number of naked men, their dicks slapping her face, fighting for the warmth of her mouth, images of women covered in semen, ropes of fresh semen on her face, in her eyeballs, in her mouth, images of women swallowing semen, spitting semen into another woman's mouth, gurgling semen, slurping semen out of a glass cup.

The images I seek out are scientific. The images I seek out are literary. The images I seek out contain knowledge. The images I seek out are purely platonic. The images I seek out own my sexuality. The images I seek out are just words. The images I seek out are not alive, they cannot be, images should not have the power to make me feel so

How to Write a Country Song

1. Everything rhymes. 2. Verse, chorus, verse, chorus, bridge, chorus. 3. **DO NOT** use the following words: sex, body, fuck, desire, ache, naked, panties, erection, hard-on, pubic hair, foreplay, cum, anal, anus, spread, lick, dick, cunt, vagina, cock, penis, pussy, porn, text message, sext, masturbate, vibrator, dildo, threesome, gangbang, group sex, gay, lesbian, tits, boobs, breasts, balls, ball sack, foreskin, flaccid, nipples, suck, missionary, doggie style, penetration, insert, condom, STD, HIV, AIDS, hand job, blow job, rim job, boob job, S&M, whip, tease, touch, taste, orgasm, jizz, squirt, scissor, rub, sperm, swingers, deep throat, finger fuck, facial, Fascism, subjectivity, objectivity, female desire, Oedipal, Electra, anorexia, mythological, media, ethical, rape, rapist, victim blaming, slut shaming, pregnancy, abortion, birth control, human rights, civil rights, equality, feminist, femininity, silence, repression, gender roles, hypermasculinity, female irrepressibility, experimentalism, existentialism, nihilism, symbolism, Freudian, debasement, punishment, violence, domestic violence, open relationships, alternatives, polygamy, atheism, agnosticism, erectile dysfunction, aging, loss of sex drive, monstrous, female monster, vagina dentata, appetite, grotesque, womb, hymen, hysterical, patriarchy, pimp, whore, madame, prostitution, capitalism, sexuality, surveillance, performance, male gaze, female object, fertility, menstruation, period blood, tampons, leaking, spilling, overflow, excess, emotions, ugliness, refusal, consent, control, power, master's tool, master's house, theory, poetry, progress, public, pubic, personal, politics, proof, subvert, authority, revolution, race, racism, artist, art.

Chattahoochee Sung By Alan Jackson

I learned how to swim and learned who I was
A lot about livin' and a little 'bout love

Country music is the river I rode

I bathed in its beer-and-semen shores

met the female objexxxts of my dreams

licked mud from the soles of their feet,

my tongue the fish between their toes

I swallowed, made them shine

they led me to my manhood

then I became a woman

then a dim body in a bed

then again a girl

when country music was done with me

I was limping naked in the woods,

a tattoo of a heart

where my heart should have been

and now here I am

shimmering

in the ugly trespass

Figure 1.

The heroine. The big-red. The girl/boy-child (me). Addictions in place. REBA IN REAL LIFE. Preparations were made early on to be the best cuntry object there ever was.

When I tell people I grew up watching porn, they seem surprised. Women often say they don't watch porn. Although didn't we all grow up with the Internet—as the Internet grew up—from one hundred free hours of AOL on a disk, to today. The Internet is our sibling, bad egg, incestuous desire.

> (The failure of the Internet. The failure of the addict. The failure of the body to orgasm. The failure of porn. The failure of endless connections. The failure of country music. The failure of feminism. The failure of fucking. The failure of being fucked. The failure of my country music songwriting dreams. The failure of this text. The failure of the confession. The failure of the penis. The failure of the cunt.)

Or maybe I went to Nashville because, as the cuntry object, I had to go all the way. I had to follow my objecthood to the birthplace of the songs themselves, the birthplace of the image of boots and cutoff jeans and big boobs and big hair. I had to go there to have a cowboy therapist in Wranglers with a handlebar moustache prove that I can set a boundary and men can stay where I put them. In collaborative songwriting, I had to have my own voice taken away to know how much I needed to speak. I was raised a cuntry object, so I went into the cunt, gaping on the screen, and into the cunt, sickly weak joke of our century, and into the cunt, slick pulsing entrance that I cup with a hand even now, and into the cunt, matted and good and voiced.

My therapist during my one year in Nashville encouraged me to think of myself as a "goddess." To draw boundaries. To not let someone cross my boundaries—become physically intimate—before they had become emotionally intimate. To protect myself. To not be treated as an object.

It was Gestalt therapy, so he made me do a lot of physical exercises—I stood on a lot of chairs. He wanted me to feel tall, big, to take up all the space in the room.

He put tape on the floors; he liked that as a physical representation of boundaries. And rope: I stood on a chair, swinging a piece of rope like a lasso. I practiced saying out loud: DON'T COME ANY CLOSER. Swing swing the lasso. I practiced saying out loud: DON'T HIT ON ME. Swing swing the lasso. I practiced saying out loud: ANGER IS NOT PRETTY and I had to start over because I was stuffing the lasso down my throat and gagging to look good.

What The Cowgirls Do Sung By Vince Gill

I love it when they let their hair down
And dance real close to you

I classify as 90scountry cowgirl dreamfuck landscapethrill

have long hair, big and bounce, have smile, thin limbs

learned everything I could: to remove excess, play

for service, pose dainty, fawn, touch while talking

how to apply the chemicals then blot for beachy subtlety

as I grew wrinkled aged and worried I already knew

to bodystuff into the puppet of my past, just waiting now

with the beauty knife— how to affect *the blank expression*

of truly contemporary beauty— for the next fist to enter,

animate me into the life I have prepared for

I don't believe I had any innocence to be stolen before the Internet arrived. I don't believe I ever fucked the Internet. I don't believe the Internet ever loved me. I do believe the Internet is the best lover I've ever had. The Internet publishes my words, my photos, my life, and strokes my hair when I am sad and lonely. The Internet does not judge me. The Internet gives me plenty of space. The Internet answers my questions and makes suggestions and shows me what the future could look like and does every dirty thing I want it to.

My sister says she grew up believing that all men, if given the opportunity, would want to fuck her. Even Jesus. Even Jesus would fuck her. My sister and I looked at porn from the beginning of the Internet until now.

The Internet now is a lot of selfies, a lot of images of women, taken by women and taken by men. The Internet now is a lot of free porn, a lot of videos. It is short bursts of information on a scrolling screen. The Internet is no longer chat rooms. The Internet is no longer web cams. The Internet is some blogs. The Internet is some art, but mainly abject feelings. The Internet now is a monster that I blame. The Internet now is the reason I was ruined. And who else is ruined. Everyone. We are the ruined, the owned, the selfied, the lost, we are the failures, the narcissists, we framed ourselves in an image and put it on the Internet for the world to see.

I mean, we framed the worst parts of ourselves and the Internet said let me hold you and this tenderness gets us off.

Dead Dog Country Song

Do you have a dog? he typed.
I typed yes.
He typed go up to the dog and spread your legs and let him lick you it will feel so good.
I typed ok.
I looked at the dog.
I typed oh yes it feels good.
Now what do you want me to do?
I had told him eighteen but I was really thirteen.
Now what do you want me to do?
He typed touch yourself and pretend it is me touching you.
He typed I have such a big dick it will feel so good inside you.
I typed okay, I typed ummmmmm ohhhh yeahhhh to say that I was touching myself and that I was thinking of him and his big dick that I did not ever want to see because those things scared me but really I was just rotating my hips against my fingers pressed to the outside of my jeans and what if my parents walk in right now I'm right here in the living room and it felt good and it felt wrong and I moved my hips in little circles right there in the living room chair facing the family computer and I felt dirty and I felt good and I felt wrong but I did it I did it until I felt good good enough.

I also looked at pictures especially of women. Always careful to delete the browser history and I looked at pictures. Especially of women. The night my mom and dad asked me have you been looking at porn on the Internet again? The night I ran to my room crying. When my mom came in I told her how I looked at pictures of women because I needed to know what a woman looked like, I was no curves no period no boys interested at all and I was doing it to compare myself to the pictures of women because I had to. I said I quit dance. I said I hate my body, I have nothing I am just sticks and bones I cannot stand to watch myself in the videos of our dances onstage I just flit around like a feather it looks so stupid.

I said I hate my body I said I quit dance I said no more porn. Of course there is that, there is still all that. And the dog died but nothing else has changed there is still that.

The First Country Song

In the rock gut core I entered the inside of my dream:

I forayed into the Nashville country music industry

carrying a naked snarl

I wore my vagina like a backpack

folded my dick like an origami cowboy hat

nothing I say sounds like the right thing to say

 but if I walk with a swagger I can please anyone

I keep making mistakes so I think I'll just keep making them

fucking the 21-year-old was a bad idea but I liked it

letting him cum on my face was a bad idea but I liked it

I wonder how he felt, how he had to act so good

when someone ten years older said I want you to hurt me

nothing I say sounds like the right thing to say

he kissed me in the bar on the patio in the rain

at the next bar, a doublewide trailer,

he put his fingers in the waist of my jeans

pulled my hips, I said, let's get a cab

he looks like a doll, or my ex-boyfriend

is this a country song

I am using him to get fucked

the way the 35-year-old boys won't fuck me

the 35-year-old boys with their limp dicks

that only last ten seconds

the 21-year-old has stamina,

he slides me to the edge of the bed

pushes his hand on my chest hard enough

my collarbone bruises the next day

I mean, is this a country song?

I touch the bruise and the pain sparks like a trophy

My therapist said clearing the throat indicates there is something you need to say. I'm clearing my throat but I'm also growling: to threaten, to scare you away.

CUNFESSION, or: THE CUNTRY OBJECT SPEAKS!:

I am trying to quit. But this is about failure.

I browse RedTube. I sometimes accidentally say RedTube in conversations when I mean to say RedBox, and like to see who notices, who knows. After I have browsed the basic offerings, the pages and pages of new porn videos since my last visit (two weeks ago), I use the search feature. I search for "old and young." I search for force. After I have watched hours of videos, I touch my clit for a few seconds, and force takes me by the throat into the darksweet corner of my own mind.

Figure 2.

The cuntry object has to be a good one—a very good girl. The cuntry object has to be danceable, must be willing to tremble and fake. She is the most fun, an unexpected fill. Pucker and pokeable. Easily packaged, easily arriving. Applaud her performance. The cuntry object has to be dirty, trash(y): lipstick, mud-covered tires, beer bottles, tight jeans, always an open hole making an O sound and it slides right in.

I let my imagination lead me along the pages of the porn site. I browse, click on suggestions at the bottom of each video. I look at BDSM, girls tied up, hit, face-fucked, gang-banged. But the image is always so obviously fake. The girls legally required to appear on camera afterwards, clean and smiling, in a bathrobe to hide the body, saying they had a really great time. They had a really great time. Giggling. I cannot watch this part. I have to look away.

Look, I do want you to read this, though. I mean, I think you can help. How do the words make you feel? Are you a cuntry object, like me? Or have you refused to look/listen? If not, what are you listening to, what are you looking at, how do you get out of your too-white lineage, who is looking at your selfies, WHO CARES ABOUT YOUR BODY IF IT'S NOT—

I'm sorry.

That was impolite.

Shameless Sung By Garth Brooks

I'm shameless when it comes to lovin' you
I'll do anything you want me to

Garth Brooks with a ball gag

Garth Brooks in leather shorts and suspenders

bound at the wrists and ankles with rope

you can be a dominatrix

Garth Brooks won't mind

he wants you to spit on him

he wants to make you feel his love

and he wants to feel your love

like a clothespin on a clit

you can put all five fingers inside his love

twist your fist in a little, too

you can lead him on a leash to your love

he'll lick it up

and you are not alone, Garth Brooks

we all want to be beaten and broken

to rub the pain 'til it bursts

into 3D, right off the page

into every open mouth

I start looking at cum shot videos, bukake: girls' faces covered in globs of semen. A boy told me they are called "ropes." A "three-roper." It gets to where I'm watching a girl tied down, and a man holds her eyelid open as another comes on her eyeball. Then the other eyeball. Soon a group of men are coming on her eyes. Then another man holds an open face-mask, a bowl, around her eyes. They keep ejaculating on her, the mask gathering everything in, on top of her eyes. Her eyes hidden by cum, creamy yellow in the bowl. Someone tells her to open her eyes; she obeys. You only see the spikey tips of her fake black eyelashes poking out of a sea of cum.

I *said*: She obeys.

Fancy Sung By Reba McEntire

She said just be nice to the gentlemen, Fancy,
They'll be nice to you

Fancy has a gun and I don't mean a *real* gun

a man has a gun and I *do* mean a penis

Fancy wields power in the shape of a girl

in the shape of a hole

which is a place you stuff dollar bills and semen

I remember Reba as Fancy,

singing at the Hollywood Bowl

I remember meeting Reba backstage

where she was less impressive than Fancy's feats

and her hair loomed large

over the family in our photo op

Reba's red gigantic hair

and Fancy's red velvet dress

were the bridges we crossed

to get to the beds we laid down on

the men looming over us

the hope in our hearts

to get out

get uptown

make mama proud

be nice

be nice

be nice

to the man

to the gun

to the things he can fill you with

Daddy's Money Sung By Ricochet

She's got her daddy's money, her mama's good looks
More laughs than a stack of comic books

(It is assumed that you have a mother and a father. You have a mother and a father, right? You know who your real mother and your real father are, right? You are American you are not illegal, right? It is *unattractive* to not be American. It is *unattractive* to not be attractive. Be attractive. Your mother should be attractive your mother should love you white. Your father should be your real spermseed beginning, not a sperm donor and God Bless the Snowflake Adoptions (prayer hands). It's not American not country to be biracial. You are white. You are white. If you are country you should probably be white but if not we can work around it (Hootie) (Leadbelly in the Nashville Songwriters Hall of Fame). Country is a mother and a father and the lineage is white pavement. And the lineage is no bodies hanging in the trees. And the lineage is not a mother and a mother OHNO! country is not a father and a father OHNO! country is ONE thing: that you have a mother and a father that you were born in America that the mother and the father are both American that the baby was born from those two people that gender is two Arctic poles we cling to and no world exists in the middle. Get your mother get your father get your gun strap your gun to your body like a good hard dick that doesn't ruin anything only creates creates creates grate your girl body against your womb your womb ready to find a man to be the father you can be the mother you MUST be a mother so find a father a suitable father the child you make must be a cuntry object is white straight attractive wet open and

Country Song of Thanks

Thank you to the man in Las Vegas who ripped my tampon out and went down on me anyway who waited who didn't put it in me when I said no let's wait till you come out to California since I was a virgin and of course he did not know that I was a virgin he said ok I will wait till I come out to California and we didn't even exchange phone numbers when I left. Thank you to the man on the plane ride home from Las Vegas who held my hand and touched my leg and wasn't mad at me when I took my hand away mad enough to find me during my layover like I was afraid of hiding in the bathroom. Thank you to the high school biology teacher who went to jail for fucking a student the year after I graduated. Thank you to the boys I led on and lay beside or on top of and rubbed against or dry humped vigorously and did not intend to fuck. Thank you to the fathers of my friends. Thank you to the boys who walked me to my car late at night in the dark to protect me from other boys. Thank you to my father thank you to my uncles thank you to the friends of my father the friends of my sister and the friends of my mother. Thank you to the boys I loved. Thank you to the boys I didn't love. Thank you to strangers. Thank you to the seventy-year olds who I danced with enough times in a row that they got a hard-on and mentioned it. Thank you to the professors who didn't shut the doors to their offices. Thank you to the boys who saw me walking wearing that outfit like a real slut. Thank you to the boys who saw me dancing that way like a real slut. Thank you to the boys who heard me talking that way like a real slut. Thank you to the boys who slept in my bed thank you to the boys who slept on my sofa thank you to the boys who slept in a hotel room a tent a train car with me. Thank you to the boys who drove to the bar to pick me up when I was too drunk and dropped me off at my apartment. Thank you to the employers the customers the landlords the neighbors the doctors the dentists the priests the babysitters' boyfriends. Thank you to the students who were older than me who were younger than me who liked me who hated me because I turned them in for plagiarism. Thank you to the boys who took me to high school dances to prom to dinner to the beach to coffee to drinks who I didn't know whose last names I didn't know who I had just met who I had known for years who laid me down in the sand who dug me into the sand who pressed against me hard in the back of a truck on a car seat standing up in a bathroom in a bed laying down against a door in boat in a pool in a zoo in a field on the steps of a public place in a strange apartment in a city I did not know. Thank you that the worst image is the way the blood dripped down my leg when I went to the bathroom after he had ripped my tampon out and how I thought for one moment that I had been because there was blood from some wound and the blood from this wound was running down my thigh until I realized it was menstrual blood so I wiped it up with tissue and put my pants back on and left the room and was not raped.

Trashy Women Sung By Confederate Railroad

Too much whiskey and too much rouge
Gets me excited, leaves me feelin' confused

If you think I won't dance in that trashcan

I'm getting in the trashcan

the dirt in my bones

I'm dancing in the rot and gut of the bloodbath

the eyeliner, the lipstick,

the sticks I lip and tongue

I was taught to lick the grime and scum

to writhe for the one and other eye

the highest spikes beneath my heel

the most red slice between my legs

to gash and heal, to rent

the filth inside of me

you will have to get in it, too

Figure 3.

What makes a good cuntry object is a hook, is the hook in the eye that she stares at you with. Fondle the utensils, kitchen appliances, push-up bra, vacuum cleaner nozzle—your accoutrements. Fondle the physical power of the man over the woman. The men are hunters. Guns swinging, guns hard and erect as a spoon in her sweetpink.

I Feel Lucky Sung By Mary Chapin Carpenter

Lyle Lovett's right beside me
With his hand upon my thigh

I was thirteen when a group of six high school girls

danced to this song in our recital

wore bathrobes over sequined leotards, sat on stools

dropped robes at the chorus

I remember: shoulders

I remember: yes

throwing off clothes,

lithe strutting in shiny flecks

meant lucky

we were a lucky audience

I still remember all six of their names

Lyle Lovett and Dwight Yoakam glaring and stroking

were nothing but words

compared to the way those six girls shimmied

out of bedclothes

and into my undressed dreams

When I was in high school, I would walk into a male friend's bedroom, met by a group of guys watching a porn VHS tape. I would sit down, watch, shielding my eyes behind spread fingers. When I was in college, I would walk into a male friend's dorm room, met by a group of guys watching Internet porn. I would sit down, watch, pretending to be disgusted.

When I was in college, I would watch Internet porn in my dorm room, hoping my roommate would not walk in. I could not be found out. And I wasn't.

Working 9 To 5 Sung By Dolly Parton

Workin' 9 to 5
What a way to make a livin'

We tapdanced on black wooden briefcases

I was twelve

I was a good tap-dancer

we tapped on top of, then beside, the fake briefcases

I was scared of Dolly Parton's boobs

my sister had large boobs at fourteen

so I called her Dolly Parton, Junior

she called me Somalia Child

I watched the other girls grow boobs

right in front of my eyes

one pair grew straight out like tin cans!

like paper snakes in a peanut jar!

we shuffled onstage carrying briefcases

like we had work to do

I had no work

I could only stare

I was a blind side scuff, a drawback, a ball change

the only one left so far behind

Rock My World (Little Country Girl) Sung By Brooks & Dunn

All the other girls in school give her dirty looks
She got an A in math and never cracked a book

She is sex dripping off a gearshift

she learned young how to man

the automatic grief machine

she flashed her cunt exiting the car

only it was the nineties so hers

was a hairy brown blow

we cheered

this was back

when it was all

so new to us

In high school, because it was 2001, I shaved off all my pubic hair. At first my girlfriends and I just shaved the edges but then the Brazilian took over the porn world and word traveled fast if you didn't remove it all. If you had a "bush." So in my boy-shaped body, before anyone ever touched me, I removed any trace of becoming a woman.

XXX's and OOO's (An American Girl) Sung By Trisha Yearwood

Got a picture of her momma in heels and pearls
She's gonna make it in her daddy's world

Are you dressed in red white and blue?

are you a comfortable canal?

are you willing to accept the loneliness

that is O! heaved into you?

are you willing to not judge the size of the (oh)

loneliness?

nor the girth?

not even the occasionanal bend?

WELCOME!

this is what it takes to make it here

XXX we are all very eager to look

and O touch

The Fireman Sung By George Strait

Everybody'd like to have what I got
I cool 'em down when they're smolderin' hot

You have a hose

you swing your hose like a tusk

you run with your hose ready

toward the biggest hottest house fires

a woman has a cunt for a house

so now it all makes sense

sometimes you like to sleep in the house

all curled up like a dead baby mouse

sometimes the woman's other house, her mouth

is on fire and that one must be sprayed down, too

phew!

thank you for doing your job, Fireman

there is no such thing as a Firewoman

(we know what that's called)

Figure 4.

The cuntry object must be willing to fuck. There is no other way to say this. But don't say it—don't mention the word, the acts. The cuntry object loves babies, children, but her babies are plastic miniature replicas. There is no other way to say this. There can be no threat of the grotesque pregnant female body, engorged, enlarged with the risk of life. If you bleed on his sheets: you're dead.

John Deere Green Sung By Joe Diffie

In John Deere Green on a hot summer night
He wrote Billy Bob Loves Charlene

The cool girl is the one who wins

wins Billy Bob of course

which is also a metaphor for marriage—

when we say marriage

we don't mean a cage!

we mean a meadow!

of flowers!

flowers that enter you gently and often

that wrap you in tender embrace

nuzzle you to orgasm with their dusty soft centers!

this is the meadow of monogamy

this is where you will bask naked

in your lover's golden pollen seed

to get there, you must never complain

go to the meadow

he will meet you there

Callin' Baton Rouge Sung By Garth Brooks

Such a strange combination
Of a woman and a child

She is the space between a hotel bed and the wall

she is slats across a cheap bench

she is a young girl unaware of the pubes snaking out from her swimsuit

while the other kids at the pool party laugh

she is the pubes

she is their wild snaking

and he is a middle-aged trucker with greasy hands

we couldn't look away

Jolene Sung By Dolly Parton

> *Your voice is soft like summer rain*
> *And I cannot compete with you, Jolene*

Jolene was like, Come here Sugartits

and he was like, but I have a girlfriend

and Jolene was like, I want your cock

and he was like, but I'm a woman

so he became a man

No one can compete with Jolene, really

it was hairy tunneling in synch

a karaoke of bursting orgasms

cuntsongs he crooned into her country

then she said, my vagina map

is pointing me in the other direction

he said, my vagina compass always points North

so he came back to me, described it all in detail

and even now I feel tight tingling below

when he moans her name at night

Something In Red Sung By Lorrie Morgan

The guaranteed number to knock a man dead,
I'm looking for something in red.

Emerald enters you and it feels good

here is a neon vibrator

this one is fuchsia

the colors mean you can see them

mean they won't get lost in your wine jug holes

you could use a paintbrush but it probably won't hit the right spots

too narrow

you could use the bristles and cuntpink paint

to cover over all this purple and brown

the ugly parts don't look like porn

won't woo the man

won't break the penis heart

Figure 5.

The cuntry object chokes. Gagging and drooling signify youth, fresh naiveté, submission. She submits. She stuffs her holes, and the stuffed holes speak for her, and she is trained to understand the difference. The cuntry object swallows the load, swallows what she is fed. Plays with what she is given. And she looks good doing it. She really does.

Pickup Man Sung By Joe Diffie

There's just somethin' women like
About a pickup man

This is my childhood trauma

I was already a dead body in the room

I was actually *that* drunk

they slung me like a hammock

the object was picked up

the girl "claims to have been raped"

it was time to prove

he was a man

he was drunk

I don't know what I was thinking

they were all—

>   *Some girls don't like boys like me.*

>   *Aw, but some girls do.*

I've never been raped, but there have been times I did not say no firmly, or loudly, or with enough conviction. I let myself be persuaded. Both times, I had verbally drawn the boundary—no sex!—and the man answered by rolling a condom down his dick—in case I changed my mind—because he *thought I wanted to*—

or did I? There is such a thin line between what you might think you want—the rape fantasy, the gangbang, abuse, to be degraded—

and what you don't want—rape—force—to be unvoiced—to have your own decision about your body plowed over, ignored—to have someone else make the decision to enter—

A Little Too Late Sung By Tanya Tucker

When you walked in, I shoulda walked out
But it's a little too late to do the right thing now

I walked into the gangbang and I was like, Oh shit

I saw the camera and I was like, Oh fuck

but it was too late

I felt his mustache on my leg

I felt their hands on my neck

I felt their dicks in my throat

but it was too late

you know a boy likes you when he _____

you know you like a boy when you _____

I hate to write this. I hate to think that anyone would know my secrets, to think that anyone would judge me. Or worse, that anyone would think they could cure me. That their dick, fingers, mouth, moves, plan of action, would be the thing to fix my dirty habit.

I'm writing because there have to be others. I'm writing because I like the way I look when I am skinny and objectified as a beautiful woman.

If I could, I would say please don't look.

I watch "Dr. Piss"—with his thick German accent—fuck girls who pretend to be patients in his white hospital room. I watch him pee into their mouths, vaginas, and assholes, held open with a speculum. It's disgusting, of course: I witness the spectacle, the excess, of the taboo sex act. I am witness to the vulgarity.

Porn is the ultimate sterile act. Every attempt to dirty it—with bodily fluids, with pain, with the appearance of force—has the same sanitized result. There are no smells, no tastes, no textures. No awkward sounds or queefs or blood or STDs or pregnancy scares or bodies slick with sweat or sour breath or bad touches.

I position myself as a voyeur. The filters, the lens, the glass screen—

the tape on the floor, the lasso in my hand—

the page, the poem—

all create distance between me and the thing I am afraid of.

I can go weeks or months without watching porn, and can feel very good about that, only to ruin my progress with binges that last all afternoon. Then I was in my parents' house in California. The Internet connection is very slow. Excruciatingly slow. A post on my Tumblr dashboard brought me an image and a name: Faye Reagan. It was like falling in love.

Faye Reagan, what are you doing in this world? Faye Reagan is freckled and red-haired, milk and cookies and puffy pink-tipped holes.

I've never had a crush on a porn star before. I objectify her, project onto her. She is a wealth of images and openings that I can observe from a distance, from the safety of my screen.

After one afternoon with Faye Reagan in California, I am sober again. Quitting. My ethics will outlast my body, or whatever it is in my mind that makes me crave the images.

Weeks later, I spend three hours in my Nashville apartment, beginning with Faye Reagan having sex with an older woman.

I've never wanted fucking to hurt for the other person. What I don't understand is the violence. What I don't understand is the desire to create physical pain, to ruin, to harm, to pound, to demolish, to obliterate, to rip, to gash, to fuck. I've been a cushion. A welcoming canal, a soft place. My vagina, mouth. I've been twisted, pushed, pulled, contorted, spread, held down, gagged, choked, and fucked. I've been a place to catch the cum: face, ass, vulva, hormone-muzzled uterus, breasts, stomach, mouth, throat, hair, back.
A landing. A map to a certain country.

Old Flames Have New Names Sung By Mark Chesnutt

There's a lot of girls in town
Who've tied the knot and settled down

The girls stay home, we know that

we know the girls never leave

the boys leave, they leave

the boys leave the girls who are waiting at home

who haven't left town, who married

who knot themselves to home

who knife out children like sliced skin

the girls stay home

the boys leave

the girls stay home to knot and wife

and weave the same endless woven rug

the boys leave

the girls stay home, waiting

the boys leave, they leave, they leave

the girls stay home, waiting for you to return

save them, untie them, stitch them

chain them

to your turnstile heart

Country Song of Regret

This is a country song about regret

a friend bit my arm, both arms, hard

while I laughed and pushed his face away

I giggled and tried not to embarrass him

I am often concerned with not embarrassing a man

doing inappropriate things to me

for example I let a married friend kiss me

for example when I was nineteen

I let a man hold my hand on an airplane

he told me about his wife and baby

and then he asked to hold my hand

I said, Yes

I imagined a flight attendant would come to my rescue

but none did

a friend said, You let men do whatever they want to you

this is a country song about

how I let men do whatever they want to me

the bruises lasted more than a week

my left arm with three circles where his teeth hit skin

the colleague whose dick I sucked in my bedroom,

who barely touched my body

who gagged me so my eye makeup ran onto the bedspread

but still I put him in my mouth

all the way, far back as I could

I cried when he left my apartment

this is a country song about

how little I have learned

Figure 6.

The cuntry object is happy to please, happy to keep the house clean, happy to be drunk, happy to slide inside the truck, happy to slide in the dildo, happy to gobble the dick down, happy to giggle, happy to lick pussy, happy to linger in the gaze, happy to dirty the sheets, happy to dribble cum into the woman's mouth, happy to fuck the father, happy to fuck the mother, happy to be the babysitter, happy to fuck the old folks, happy to stay young, happy to wear pigtails, happy to pretend to be much younger than she ever was.

Maybe It Was Memphis Sung By Pam Tillis

What was I s'posed to do, standin' there lookin' at you
A lonely boy far from home

I am not from the South

I am from the West

the South is what I succumbed to

an allegory about the West:

a woman was swimming in the Pacific Ocean

wearing a black wetsuit

she came very close to some cute seals

and was eaten by a shark who mistook her for a seal

this is a true story

this is how you die in the West:

by trying too hard

in the South, you don't die

because no one tries too hard

things just happen: trip

and you land on a strange boy's hard cock

Angry Woman Country Song

I displaced myself to prove I am a real woman

I displaced myself to prove I am a real artist

I burned down my house, I am inside of a flame

are you inside of a flame, too?

but is the flame red with regret?

I am being eaten alive by regret

I left a place, unstuck myself from home

unpeeled myself from a comfort to see what grows

my life was a glass jar of fireflies

it wasn't enough so I threw the jar against a wall

now I'm picking up all the dead fireflies

their bulbs burst on impact, their lights went out

did you do this, too?

did you crush your glass jar,

your tiny lights?

are you afraid?

I wasn't afraid to burn my house down,

I lit the match eagerly

threw the jar with all my might, laughing

now I am standing in the low heat trying to eat all the men

when threatened,

one way for the animal to protect itself

is to become vicious

I have become so mad I will do

whatever the boys say to do

so I can hate them afterwards

look what they made me do

femme fatales are my favorite fatales

a dangerous man is just the oldest news

Should've Been A Cowboy Sung By Toby Keith

He just stole a kiss as he rode away
He never hung his hat up at Kitty's place

Kitty is neither bandit nor heroine

I am looking back at a man

looking back at the woman

he didn't choose to stick around for

women and their wilderness

their lack

today the girls parade their wild

wearing all the same clothes

wedge heels, stick legs wobbling

photographing and posting,

riding the slow turtle of the self

and the TV shows them

and the Internet shows them

and the radio shows them

lots of pretty women

We should've been cowboys

we should've learned to ride something

more veiny than a keyboard,

camera phone, credit card

in the tight hot cells of our hearts

what we wanted wasn't kiss and vow

but a way to shatter,

then steer

Figure 7.

Be the cuntry object. Let the camera watch as you perform your duties. The cuntry object does it for the money. The cuntry object does not do it for the money. The cuntry object was raised poor, was raised in an affluent suburb of LA. No— the cuntry object has no history, no family—she only looks good as she takes it. She needs to be filled. Fill her. She does it for love. She does it 4 luv. She does it for the fucking, love.

I Love The Way You Love Me Sung By John Michael Montgomery

I love the way your eyes dance when you laugh
And how you enjoy your two hour baths

As a girl, I masturbated against the bubbles

I slid and banged around the walls of the tub like a seal

like a penis in the porcelain

I was two mouths, sucking

water in and out, choking

I impaled myself on the spout

my vagina was big as the sink stopper

sputtering and gasping for air

I drowned in the bathwater

I emerged a woman

and toweled off

"COUNTRY" WITHOUT THE O:

I should note that the times I've come with a real person—I've had roughly twenty male partners, so I'm just counting vaginal penetration—if I had to count oral sex with men, I'd be shit out of luck, since I've used blowjobs habitually to fend off sex—and three female partners, who I count, even though with women it's only been oral sex (and this is a double standard, I know)—I should note that although I've had these partners, I have only had an orgasm from four people.

When I come from porn, my body is rigid, quiet; the feeling a little burst. Easy satisfaction.

When I try to come from others, I arch, sway, moan, ache, shiver, thrust, dissect myself. Pull the person against me. Perform, focus. And fail. And fail.

Independence Day Sung By Martina McBride

Word gets around in a small, small town
They said he was a dangerous man

A boy and his gun

the gun and its fist

the fist and the cunt

the cunt and the camera and the fist

the violet attack in artificial light

the sparkling blood

the festive bruise

the death

a girl and her death

a girl and her banged velour

her leather economy

her dense shift

the girl's lawlessness

the law of the boy's fingers around her throat

crushed glass of the globe

cue the fireworks

I must be honest now. Let me remove my masks to say how I have failed. Let me draw out my knives, my bombs, my phallic gun. When I am armed like this—shoulders heavy with artillery, hips saddled by ammo, explosives ticking away—the words so clear, nothing hidden by abstractions, the narrative, is this even good writing?—when I am armed like this, I know how *unattractive* it is.

Like when my father asked me to wear flats. "When you wear those high heels, you're such a *big* girl."

I know how large and fearsome I am in my honest desires. Isn't it at least a little exciting for you? To see the failure?

There was one time when I came without thinking of, or looking at, porn. *One* time. I was making out with a girl, a beautiful poet—we'd been hooking up in grad school, my first experiences with a woman—and she was on my sofa. I was on top of her, rubbing against her leg. Just kissing, rubbing, breast, mouth—and I came, unexpectedly, without even trying. We stopped. I couldn't go on—so embarrassed that, for once, I was not in control. Not a failure. My body had made up its own mind.

I've never been able to answer if that orgasm stemmed from her, from my sexual desire, or that the moment simply *looked like porn*.

Internet Porn Country Song

AOL came in the mail, on a disc: 100 hours free trial

the Internet arrived

he brought his laptop to you, said let's look together

so you looked together

you Googled sex, the first thing you searched for was sex

you saw a penis for the first time

gigantic and ruby red in the huge cock way

you were scared

you cybered

I mean, you had cyber sex

you wanted to know the words, didn't you

a penis hammered into a vagina

you should have looked away

you looked together and he touched you

you walked into the boys' dorm room

and they were looking at porn

your roommate walked into your dorm room

and you were looking at porn

you quickly closed the screen closed the laptop flipped to another tab

you erased the computer history but it didn't work

your parents caught you

Girls Gone Wild played in the background at a party

you couldn't look away

you rubbed against the floor while your roommate wasn't looking

the iPhone arrived

he took photos of you on his iPhone

you walked naked in the forest and he took photos of you on his iPhone

there were a whole lot of people in the room

you looked together and he touched you

and you had only ever touched yourself

the man wanted to meet you

you weren't alone and you cried

you finished and you cried

you said, please erase those pictures of me

you said, that one's okay

you were afraid

you were no longer afraid

you wanted to know why it was always the looking that did it

you used to be so simple

you used to be so pure

no: when was it ever just you

and an open hand

you looked

you looked

someone asked you if you looked

you said, yes, I do,

and I like it

The Last Country Song

1

These country songs don't even have a chorus

these country songs have forgotten to rhyme

the listeners need a rhyme to comfort them like mothering

you should repeat the title as often as possible

this is the last country song

I could never say no and I am now the universal I

or, I tried to say no and I am now the universal I

dear country music, how are you implicated in my failures?

dear country, who to blame?

dear cunt, re-do the parts where your desire was left out

the desire of the cunt is always left out

except where I wrote it in

to fix

this is the last country song

I made mistakes because I was gathering attention

like dirt roads in a country song

I was taught this

WE ARE ALL JUST FOLLOWING DIRECTIONS

I'm not angry at anyone

what I'm saying is my boundaries are thin as a thigh gap

because part of me is in it for the win

to be the ultimate cuntry object

who is the girl in all the country songs?

she is someone I used to want to be

until I stopped listening too close to every chorus

until I disrobed the country song

and made it do all the ugly things

saw it flaccid and shivering

with blatant human needs

haven't we all been embarrassed

by the country song's desire for us?

I hovered above the country song

all my power concentrated in each thick

throbbing gob

but with so many holes,

how could any country song truly please me?

get up, country song

go take your wanting elsewhere

3

The country song had a lot to say about me

so I provided all the wrong clues

the country song gazed

so I learned to gaze back

it's rude to stare

but I do it with my cock hat on

dear women:

our many holes are bulbous tender forts

enter the monstrous feminine

it's the opposite of country songs

Notes

pg. 2: The second epigraph is from Katherine Angel's *Unmastered: A Book on Desire, Most Difficult to Tell* (Farrar, Straus and Giroux 2013).

pg. 5: The italicized lines are from David Abram's *The Spell of the Sensuous: Perception and Language in a More-Than-Human World* (Vintage 1997).

pg. 15: The italicized line is from Ariana Reines' *Coeur de Lion* (Mal-O-Mar 2008).

pg. 31: "Automatic grief machine" is from Kevin González' *Cultural Studies* (Carnegie Mellon Poetry Series 2009).

pg. 52: Some lines reference Louise Bogan's poem, "Women," from *Body of this Death* (Robert McBride 1923).

Acknowledgements

Thank you to the editors of the following literary magazines, where earlier versions of these poems, some with different titles, were first published: *Octopus, Eleven Eleven, Horseless Review, Tenderloin, Finery, Everyday Genius, H_NGM_N, Booth, Booth X, The Feminist Wire, Smoking Glue Gun,* and *LIT*. Thank you also to Dancing Girl Press, where two poems were originally published, with different titles, in the chapbook *Orthorexia* (Dancing Girl Press 2011).

Thank you to the following people, some of whom read versions of this manuscript, and others for your support of this project: Laura Mullen, Megan Burns, Lisa Pasold, Jenn Marie Nunes, Mel Coyle, Anne Marie Rooney, Megan McHugh, Jerika Marchan, Ben Kopel, Chelsea Hodson, Elizabeth Hall, Myriam Gurba, Rodrigo Toscano, and Arielle Greenberg.

Kristin Sanders is the author of two poetry chapbooks, *Orthorexia* (Dancing Girl Press 2011), and *This is a map of their watching me,* a finalist in the 2015 BOAAT Chapbook Competition. She has taught at Cal Poly, San Luis Obispo; Loyola University, New Orleans; Belmont University; and Louisiana State University. She is currently a poetry editor for the *New Orleans Review* and a contributing writer at *Weird Sister. CUNTRY* was a finalist for the 2015 National Poetry Series.

Trembling Pillow Press

I of the Storm by Bill Lavender

Olympia Street by Michael Ford

Ethereal Avalanche by Gina Ferrara

Transfixion by Bill Lavender

Downtown by Lee Meitzen Grue

SONG OF PRAISE   Homage To John Coltrane by John Sinclair

DESERT JOURNAL by ruth weiss

Aesthesia Balderdash by Kim Vodicka

SUPER NATURAL by Tracey McTague

I LOVE THIS AMERICAN WAY OF LIFE by Brett Evans

Q by Bill Lavender

loaded arc by Laura Goldstein

Want for Lion by Paige Taggart

Trick Rider by Jen Tynes

May Apple Deep by Michael Sikkema

Gossamer Lid by Andrew Brezna

simple constructs for the lizzies by Lisa Cattrone

FILL: A Collection by Kate Schapira and Erika Howsare

Red of Split Water a burial rite by Lisa Donovan

CUNTRY by Kristin Sanders

Forthcoming Titles:

Kids of the Black Hole by Marty Cain

If You Love Error So Love Zero by Stephanie Anderson

Feelings by Lauren Ireland

Trembling Pillow Press

Bob Kaufman Book Prize

2012: *Of Love & Capital* by Christopher Rizzo (Bernadette Mayer, judge)

2013: *Psalms for Dogs and Sorcerers* by Jen Coleman (Dara Wier, judge)

2014: *Natural Subjets* by Divya Victor (Anselm Berrigan, judge)

2015: *there are boxes and there is wanting* by Tessa Micaela Landreau-Grasmuck (Laura Mullen, judge)

2016 *orogeny* by Irène Mathieu (Megan Kaminski, judge)

www.tremblingpillowpress.com